cloverleaf books™

Holidays and Special Days

WITHDRAWN

Sarah's Passover

Lisa Bullard

illustrated by Constanza Basaluzzo

M MILLBROOK PRESS · MINNEAPOLIS

To Wendy —L.B.
To Javier and Nina —C.B.

Millbrook Press
A division of Lerner Publishing Group, Inc.
241 First Avenue North
Minneapolis, MN 55401 USA

For reading levels and more information, look up this title at
www.lernerbooks.com.

Main body text set in Slappy Inline 18/28.
Typeface provided by T26.

Library of Congress Cataloging-in-Publication Data

Bullard, Lisa.
    Sarah's Passover / by Lisa Bullard ; illustrated by
Constanza Basaluzzo.
        p.   cm. — (Cloverleaf Books holidays and special days)
    Includes index.
    ISBN 978-0-7613-5081-1 (lib. bdg. : alk. paper)
    ISBN 978-0-7613-8837-1 (eBook)
    1. Passover—Juvenile literature. I. Basaluzzo, Constanza, ill.
II. Title.
BM695.P3B85 2012
296.4'37—dc23   2011028789

Manufactured in the United States of America
2 – BP – 1/1/14

TABLE OF CONTENTS

Chapter One

It's Time for Passover!

Hi! I'm Sarah. A big holiday is coming up. It's called **Passover.** I have some important jobs to do during this holiday! Today I'm helping Mom get the house ready.

While I help, Mom reminds me why we celebrate Passover. Long ago, the Jewish people were called the **Israelites**. They were slaves in Egypt for many years. Every Passover, we remember that our people used to be slaves. We celebrate our freedom.

The Passover story tells how the Israelite slaves were set free. God sent a man named Moses to see the Egyptian king. Moses asked the king to free the Israelites. But the king said no. So God sent many troubles to Egypt. Finally, the king let the Israelites leave.

Chapter Two

Helping to Get Ready

We get the **whole house clean.** Then I clean out the regular bread and cookies. Those are some of the foods we can't eat during Passover. I help get all of them out of the house.

I brush a feather across the shelves.
That way, I don't miss even one crumb.

I'm good at finding the special Passover foods at the store. I put lots of **matzah** in the cart. Matzah is like a big cracker.

Regular bread needs time to rise before it can be baked. But the Israelites had to leave Egypt in a hurry. They didn't even have time for their bread to rise. They had to make hard, flat bread instead. It's called matzah. Now Jewish people eat matzah every year during Passover.

Crunch! We eat it instead of regular bread.

Chapter Three

The Seder

It's almost time for the **seder!** The Seder is the special dinner that starts Passover. Mom and I get the seder plate ready. I add the **egg** to the plate. Then the doorbell rings.

What special foods do families put on their seder plate?

—an egg
—a bone
—a vegetable, often parsley
—*charoset*, a mix of chopped apples and nuts
—a bitter herb
—a bitter vegetable

Charoset reminds us of the material the Israelite slaves used to make bricks. The bitter foods help people remember how hard it is to be a slave. All the foods help tell the Passover story.

Lots of relatives come for the seder. But we don't eat right away. First, we follow along in the **Haggadah.** This book tells the story of how the Israelites became free.

We say blessings and give thanks to God. I bounce in my chair.
I can't wait for my special part!

Passover is a spring holiday. It lasts for a week.

13

Grandfather breaks the middle matzah. Then he puts a piece in a napkin. **He hides it.** Later on, we'll search for it.

The hidden matzah is called the *afikomen*.

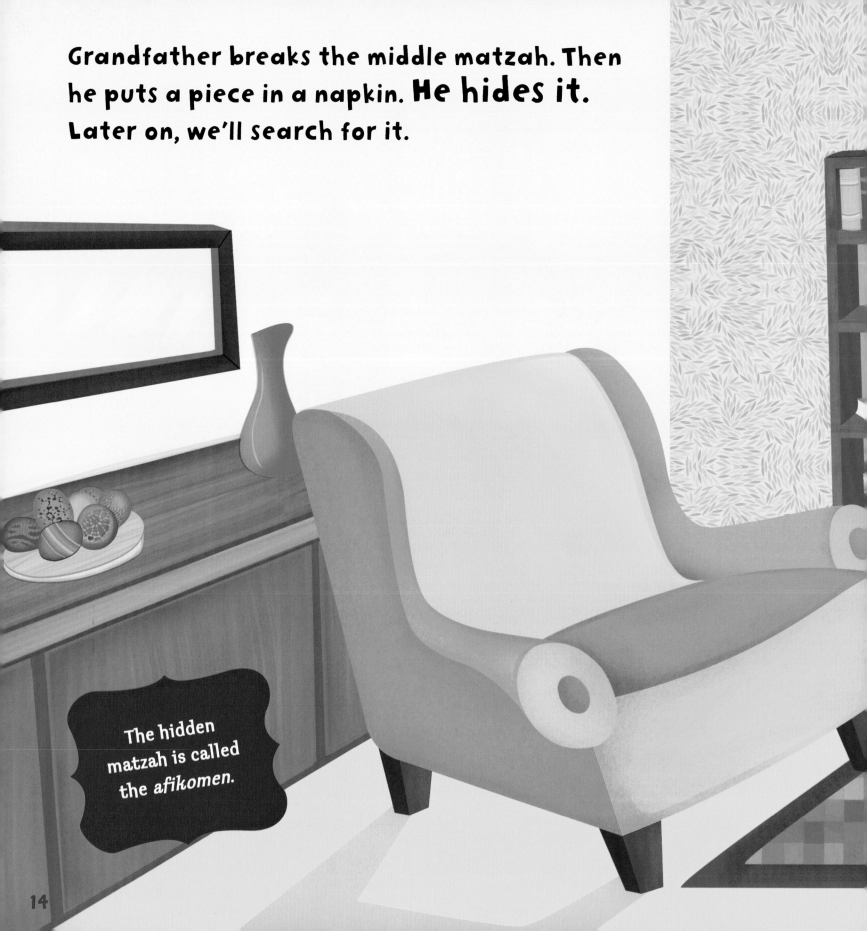

I bet I'll be the one to find it!

Sometimes, being the youngest is hard. But for the seder, being the youngest makes me special! I get to ask the **Four Questions.**

Each year at the seder, the youngest child asks the Four Questions. Sometimes the questions are sung. They ask why certain things are done at the seder. The adults at the table answer the questions by telling the story of Passover.

I start, "Why is this night different from all other nights?"

Grandfather answers my questions with stories about our people.

17

Finally, we eat. Then all the kids get to look for the **hidden matzah.** Grandfather is tricky. But I find the matzah before any of the big kids can.

I guess **I'm tricky** too! Grandfather gives me candy as a prize. Then we all **eat the matzah**.

The afikomen is the last thing eaten at the seder.

Chapter Four

Remember and Celebrate

Passover will be over in a few days. Then we'll eat regular bread again.

People have celebrated Passover for more than three thousand years. The holiday is also called Pesach. It is celebrated in countries all around the world.

But today, I eat matzah. It reminds me that our people were once slaves. It reminds me to be thankful for **freedom**.

21

Make a Passover Pillowcase

Some families lean on pillows while they eat the seder dinner. This reminds them that they are free. Free people can be comfortable. Slaves cannot!

Now you can make a special Passover pillowcase. Then you can lean on your own seder pillow.

What you need:
a white pillowcase (Get permission to draw on it!)
fabric markers
newspaper or a large piece of cardboard
a grown-up to help at the end

What to do:
1) Lay your pillowcase on a hard surface, such as a table.

2) Put the newspaper or cardboard inside the pillowcase. This will keep the colors from bleeding through to the other side.

3) Think a little before you start drawing: What would make a good picture for your Passover pillow? Maybe you would like to draw a picture from the Passover story? Or a picture of the seder plate? Or a picture of your family?

4) Use the fabric markers to draw your picture.

5) Ask a grown-up to read the directions on the markers that you use. Some kinds of markers need a grown-up to do a follow-up step, such as ironing or putting the pillowcase in the dryer.

6) Make sure your pillowcase is dry before you use it.

GLOSSARY

afikomen (AH-fee-KOH-men): a piece of matzah that is hidden during the seder and then eaten last

bitter: a taste or flavor that is sharp or even bad

celebrate: do something to show how special or important something is

charoset (hah-ROH-set): a mix that often includes chopped apples, nuts, spices, and sometimes honey

Haggadah (hah-GAH-duh): a book that tells the story of the Israelite slaves being set free. *Haggadah* means "to tell a story."

herb (urb): a plant used to flavor food

Israelites (IHZ-ree-uh-LITES): a group of people who once lived in the part of the world called the Middle East

Jewish: related to the religion called Judaism or to the people known as Jews

matzah (MAHT-sah): a hard, flat bread made from flour and water

Passover: a Jewish holiday celebrating the Israelites' escape from slavery in Egypt

Pesach (PAY-sahk): the name for Passover in the Hebrew language

seder (SAY-dur): a special Passover dinner that follows the same order every year. *Seder* means "order" in Hebrew.

slave: a person who is owned by another person and is forced to work for them without getting paid

synagogue (SIHN-uh-GAHG): the place where Jewish people worship

BOOKS

Fishman, Cathy Goldberg. *Passover.* Minneapolis: Millbrook Press, 2006.
The illustrations in this book take you through the history of Passover and how it is celebrated.

Pirotta, Saviour. *Passover.* New York: Rosen, 2008.
Check out this book for photos of a seder meal and more information about Passover.

Portnoy, Mindy Avra. *A Tale of Two Seders.* Minneapolis: Kar-Ben, 2010.
Follow along as a little girl tells the story of her many different seder celebrations, some at her mom's house, and some at her dad's.

WEBSITES

Khalikidan's Passover Seder
http://shalomsesame.org/videos/passover_seder.html
Visit this website from Shalom Sesame to watch a video about a girl named Khalikidan as she gets ready for and celebrates Passover.

Passover
http://www.chabad.org/kids/article_cdo/aid/354750/jewish/Passover.htm
This website features videos, games, and many other activities to help you learn more about Passover.

Passover Coloring Pages and Puzzles
http://www.akhlah.com/holidays/pesach/passover_coloringpages.php
Check out this website for pages you can color and Passover puzzles.

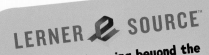

LERNER 𝑒 SOURCE™
Expand learning beyond the printed book. Download free, complementary educational resources for this book from our website, www.lerneresource.com.